Liquid

LIVE AT FIVE

—

WRITTEN BY JEFF PRIES

THOMAS NELSON
Since 1798

NASHVILLE   DALLAS   MEXICO CITY   RIO DE JANEIRO   BEIJING

Published in Nashville, Tennessee. Thomas Nelson is a trademark of Thomas Nelson, Inc.

Published in association with the literary agency of Yates & Yates, LLP, Attorneys and Counselors, Orange, California.

Thomas Nelson, Inc. titles may be purchased in bulk for educational, business, fund-raising, or sales promotional use. For information, please e-mail SpecialMarkets@ThomasNelson.com.

Unless noted otherwise, all Scripture quotations are taken from the New Century Version®. Copyright © 2005 by Thomas Nelson, Inc. Used by permission. All rights reserved.

ISBN: 978-1-4185-3353-3

Printed in China.
08 09 10 11 12 SS 9 8 7 6 5 4 3 2 1

■ CONTENTS

■ INTRODUCTION

LIQUID

Five episodes. One story.

God's Word is as true today as it was when it was written.

But for too long, we have looked at God's Word and wondered how it could possibly impact our lives. It's one thing to simply read the Bible. It's something different altogether to understand it. Far too often we read these stories about people in an ancient land, and we're left feeling flat. "What's this got to do with me?" We know in our hearts that what we're reading is true, right, and good, but we can't see any real way to apply it.

That's where *LIQUID* comes in.

LIQUID presents true-to-life stories of characters with real problems. Because what's the point in putting together a study of God's Word that doesn't deal with any of the issues we actually face? Along with each chapter in this book is a film, filled with characters that live in our world—the real world. Yet their problems and struggles mirror the same struggles found in stories in the Bible.

Jesus is the master storyteller. He helped people understand, made them contemplate, made them consider. He wasn't afraid to cut a story a couple of ways, as if he was saying, "Let me say it another way, a different way, so you can understand." He often gave answers by asking questions in return, so people would investigate, think, learn. It's how he did it, so it's why we do it. We translate ancient stories into the language of today's culture, and we ask relevant questions to help you discover the truth for yourself.

Whether you're with a small group, or simply by yourself, all we ask is that you take a deep breath, pop in the DVD, and then read through these pages and think carefully about the questions and the Scriptures. These are not questions from the SAT—they don't have definitive answers. They are designed for you to reflect upon based on your perspective. Everyone's discoveries will be different. But that's what's great about God's truth—it's one truth, but it's formed differently around each person.

It's simply about taking in, reflecting, and coming up with something useful for your life. Now at last we have an immediate, portable, relevant way to experience God's Word. A revolutionary new way to study the Bible.

LIQUID. God's Word flowing through your life.

■■ LIVE AT FIVE

Being on live TV can be a frantic, stressful time. It can bring out the best in people, and it can bring out the worst. Some rise to the occasion, and some melt under the lights. It is during these stressful times that you often really "see" people; you see where they really are and what their hearts are like.

Now throw in the live news, and you will see life—life at its best and life at its worst. In these situations, people are often surprised, taken off guard by some occurrence, and placed right into their lives, their faces, is the camera. You hear what they say; you watch what they do. Their actions and their comments speak volumes.

That's what the book of James is all about. Looking into the hearts of people, what they say, how they act. Told from the perspective of a firsthand reporter—James, the half brother of Jesus—we get a great perspective on some of life's most important issues. The book of James is about how to live life, and how to live it practically.

It's exciting, a lot like watching live TV.

CHAPTER 1: BAD DAY

I was standing in line at Starbucks this morning, and the woman in front of me could not decide what she wanted to order. First it was the caramel macchiato; then it was the white chocolate mocha; then the iced coffee, because the other two drinks had too many calories. Five drink orders later, I was still waiting for her to make up her mind. I wasn't the only one waiting, either. There were six people behind me, tapping their feet impatiently. I couldn't decide whether I wanted to scream, come along beside her and order for her, or push her out of the way as I ordered my own drink. But I waited patiently instead.

When was a time recently that you had to show restraint or patience with someone?

Play video episode now.

I'll admit that I'm an *American Idol* junkie. I only watch it because my kids love it . . . at least that's my story. But it seems like a tough show to be on. Not only do you have to bare your soul to the world, but three judges and America get to decide whether they like it or not. Talk about rejection! And then when they vote you off the show, they make you sing one last time—you know, the song everyone hated to begin with. Then they show a slide show of your progression—both the highlights and the lowlights. And then they used to play the song "Bad Day" in the background. Now, that's a bad day.

What were the struggles Natalie faced in the episode?

How did she respond?

How would you have responded?

[1] From James, a servant of God and of the Lord Jesus Christ. Greetings.

To all of God's people who are scattered everywhere in the world:

Greetings.

[2] My brothers and sisters, when you have many kinds of troubles, you should be full of joy, [3] because you know that these troubles test your faith, and this will give you patience. [4] Let your patience show itself perfectly in what you do. Then you will be perfect and complete and will have everything you need. [5] But if any of you needs wisdom, you should ask God for it. He is generous and enjoys giving to all people, so he will give you wisdom. [6] But when you ask God, you must believe and not doubt. Anyone who doubts is like a wave in the sea, blown up and down by the wind. [7-8] Such doubters are thinking two different things at the same time, and they cannot decide about anything they do. They should not think they will receive anything from the Lord.

What does the passage say about troubles and how to respond to them?

CULTURAL AND HISTORICAL THOUGHTS:

At the time he wrote this letter, James had experienced struggles and adversities, including witnessing Jesus crucified as an innocent man. He also knew Stephen, who had just been stoned for preaching the gospel. He would have seen broken families and marriages, and the persecution of Christians.

God refers to troubles and suffering throughout the Old and New Testaments, and never does he say he will take them away or that we won't experience them. Instead, God says we will not be abandoned during those times. He will provide for us, he waits to hear from us, and he will give us wisdom.

I'm reading an article about how the amount of foreclosures on houses is on the rise in the U.S. I think to myself, *What would I do if I couldn't make my house payment? What would I tell the kids, my friends, my family?* The more I think about it, the more miserable I start to feel. Not for myself, but for the people in the article. *Please, please, don't ever let that happen to my family,* I think. Then I continue to read, and the dad in the article begins talking about how their foreclosure actually brought the family together. They went from being a disconnected family to a family that bonded with each other through tough times.

How do people view troubles or struggles today?

How do they respond?

When I'm in trouble, I usually have a progression of emotions. First I get scared; then I panic; then I call for help. If no one comes, then I seek out help. Maybe I drive to a friend's house, or I ask someone at work for guidance. I'm always really calm about it, but really I'm dying inside. Trouble devastates me when I'm experiencing it. But when I look back at some of the struggles I've had, there's a major theme—trouble has always resulted in something positive. Maybe it wasn't what I thought the result should be, but somehow I grew from the experience.

What troubles are you facing in your life right now and how will you respond?

I've been watching my young sons swing a sledgehammer, breaking down the brick wall in the front yard. The sledgehammer probably weighs more that they do. I admire their tenacity, their strength at such a young age. I can't believe how long they are lasting at this task. They have probably given the wall about twenty shots. I think they like to see the brick shatter and fly. After several hours, my son stops and walks over to me, holding his hands. Just as I thought, he has two huge blisters. I told them that if they swung the sledgehammer long enough—for a few days—their hands would toughen and form calluses. Just like swinging a sledgehammer, when you have to work at something, when things are hard, it does something to you. It makes you tougher, stronger.

As you look back at the struggles in your life, how did you handle them?
How did you handle something badly? How did you handle something well?
How did it make you stronger?

Who is someone that you admire for how that person handled adversity?
What made you admire him or her?

How have the struggles in your past influenced and changed you?
For the worse? For the better?

How do struggles influence your relationship with God?
Make it better? Make it more challenging?

CHAPTER 2: TEMPTATIONS

Every night it sits there, whispering to me, calling out to me, drawing me in. I casually pass by it maybe twenty times, just living out the normal events of the evening . . . but I don't forget it's there. When the kids are in bed and my wife is in the other room, reading a book, that is when the pull becomes the strongest. And what do I do? I reach into the freezer and pull out the half gallon of ice cream—the carton that has been calling my name all night. I'll dig out about five heaping spoonfuls and put it in a bowl. Then I put it in the microwave for about twenty-five seconds, just to get it a little soft. I head to the couch to sit and enjoy my treat. Five minutes of devouring, followed by thirty minutes of guilt. When I put it back in the freezer, I whisper "Till we meet again" . . . which will probably be tomorrow night.

What food is your biggest weakness?

Play video episode now.

Temptation in the workplace. Everyone can identify. We all feel the pull. We want to get ahead, or to keep our preferred position. We want to make an impression on our boss, co-workers, the world. Maybe we sacrifice a little of our morality, or stomp over someone else to get the edge, or maybe we just look the other way when it's convenient to do so. Our jobs can sometimes bring out the worst in us. Maybe it's the pressure, maybe it's our competitive nature, maybe it's just the idea that "everyone else is doing it," and it feels like the only way to survive. In the workplace, it can be tempting to do things you know are wrong.

In the film, what temptation is Natalie facing?

What will happen if she gives in?

What will happen if she stays strong?

[12] When people are tempted and still continue strong, they should be happy. After they have proved their faith, God will reward them with life forever. God promised this to all those who love him. [13] When people are tempted, they should not say, "God is tempting me." Evil cannot tempt God, and God himself does not tempt anyone. [14] But people are tempted when their own evil desire leads them away and traps them. [15] This desire leads to sin, and then the sin grows and brings death.

[16] My dear brothers and sisters, do not be fooled about this. [17] Every good action and every perfect gift is from God. These good gifts come down from the Creator of the sun, moon, and stars, who does not change like their shifting shadows. [18] God decided to give us life through the word of truth so we might be the most important of all the things he made.

What do you learn about temptation from this passage?

As I'm sitting at the computer, a pop-up on the screen says: "See movie stars in lingerie!" I sit there and think to myself, *I wonder who it is?* It's tempting, but I don't click on it. Instead, I turn the computer off and I walk away. I haven't done anything wrong. I didn't cross the line. Temptation does that—it can come out of nowhere and try to bring us down. But being tempted doesn't mean we've done anything wrong. We can still walk away. We can still experience victory.

What is the process of desire, temptation, defeat, and victory?

Pick a few different struggles that people deal with, and break down what this process would look like for each struggle. At what point is a line crossed?

What would happen if people gave in to those temptations?

What would happen if people trusted God?

In the past, wars were fought against countries using clearly defined armies and for clearly defined results. You knew whom you were up against, you knew where they were from, you saw what flag they flew. You would either face squadrons of airplanes, a whole aircraft carrier deployment, or tank battalions. These were more conventional, formidable opponents. Now we fight battles and wars where it is hard to identify the enemy. Who is good, who is bad? Where is the opposition coming from? Why won't they show their face and stand up and fight? It can be frustrating. I want to know the enemy so I can take him straight on. That's how temptation can be. It helps to be able to identify the enemy. To know where he's coming from so you can take him head-on. You know who the enemy is, don't you?

What is an area in your life where you feel tempted but don't cross the line? Where is an area in which temptation is leading you over the line? Why do you experience strength in one area and not the other?

What are truths from the passage that can help you deal with not giving in to temptation?

I do a lot of marriage counseling, and I often find myself listening to the struggles of guys who have given in to temptation. Unfortunately, most of the temptation is in the area of sexual struggle. I ask them when they feel most vulnerable, and they usually say it is when they feel disconnected in one way or another from their wives. We all have those times when we are more susceptible to stepping over the line. We need to recognize when we are at greater risk. Whether our struggle is drinking, overspending, dealing with our anger, or looking at things we shouldn't look at, we need to recognize it so we can fight it.

What makes certain things in life more tempting than others?

How does the world work hard at trying to tempt us?

What is an area of temptation that you have overcome?
What helped you to overcome it?

When do you feel most tempted in life?

What are things you do to help deal with temptation?

CHAPTER 3: WORDS

Liquid

I'm not great at affirmations—receiving them or giving them. About a month ago I went to lunch with a bunch of my friends, and we were talking about our wives and how we need to affirm them. I decided to give it a try. I mustered up all my nerve and e-mailed my wife and told her she was beautiful. About five minutes later I got an e-mail back from her. I wondered what she was going to say back to me. Maybe she would tell me that I'm wonderful, or handsome, or a good father. Heck, I would have taken anything. Just throw me a bone! I clicked on the e-mail, and it said, "You spelled 'beautiful' wrong." It wasn't quite what I was hoping for. I guess we can all work on affirmation in some way or another.

Describe an affirmation or a great compliment that you've received.

Play video episode now.

Just a slip of the tongue—a little word here, a little word there. Leave a detail out, maybe add an embellishment to the story, a different inflection in your voice, and your words can take on a completely different meaning. Words are powerful. They can affect people in strong ways. They have the ability to cheer people up when they are having a bad day, or encourage someone when he or she is down and out. Words can also turn a celebration into an awkward moment, or hurt someone we really care about. Or even worse, they can make an innocent man look guilty.

How did you see the power of words play out in this episode?

[1] My brothers and sisters, not many of you should become teachers, because you know that we who teach will be judged more strictly. [2] We all make many mistakes. If people never said anything wrong, they would be perfect and able to control their entire selves, too. [3] When we put bits into the mouths of horses to make them obey us, we can control their whole bodies. [4] Also a ship is very big, and it is pushed by strong winds. But a very small rudder controls that big ship, making it go wherever the pilot wants. [5] It is the same with the tongue. It is a small part of the body, but it brags about great things.

A big forest fire can be started with only a little flame. [6] And the tongue is like a fire. It is a whole world of evil among the parts of our bodies. The tongue spreads its evil through the whole body. The tongue is set on fire by hell, and it starts a fire that influences all of life. [7] People can tame every kind of wild animal, bird, reptile, and fish, and they have tamed them, [8] but no one can tame the tongue. It is wild and evil and full of deadly poison. [9] We use our tongues to praise our Lord and Father, but then we curse people, whom God made like himself. [10] Praises and curses come from the same mouth! My brothers and sisters, this should not happen. [11] Do good and bad water flow from the same spring? [12] My brothers and sisters, can a fig tree make olives, or can a grapevine make figs? No! And a well full of salty water cannot give good water.

What do you learn about the tongue and its effects?

I watched the movie *Braveheart* on TV the other night. I am amazed how those guys can wield a sword. Just one piece of pounded metal in the hands of the right man can create some pretty devastating destruction. Now, you've heard that the tongue is mightier than the sword, and that is as true today as in ancient Ireland. Words can encourage or dishearten, praise or condemn, build up or destroy. Words can show love or hatred, can be truthful or deceitful, and can join people together or tear them apart. Just like any weapon, words can be sharp, cutting, and deadly.

What situations or places tend to bring out the worst or best in people's tongues?

Where have you seen the effects of someone's words?

What is a positive example? What about a negative example?

We all respond differently in different situations. Maybe situations in which you feel attacked or cornered make you fly off the handle and lose control of your mouth. I have the opposite reaction. If someone goes after me, I shut down. It's actually an area where I can control my tongue pretty well. I guess I know where my mouth would go if I let myself respond. Shutting down keeps me in control; it's my defense mechanism. Now, put me in a situation where everyone's just joking around and I'm in big trouble. I will take jokes right to the edge, just looking for a laugh. And, man, can I cross the line. I get myself in trouble, and I'm left with the only words left to say: "I'm so sorry. I didn't mean to hurt you."

What situations in your life seem to bring out the worst in your tongue?

Where in your life can you use your words in a positive way? What effect would this have on your life and on those around you?

We all say things that come back to haunt us. Words stand the test of time. Bill Clinton will never live down the line, "I didn't inhale." Just to keep it fair, George Bush Sr. said, "Read my lips." It's like squeezing toothpaste out of the tube—you can't put it back in. What's been done has been done. It's the same with our words. You can never put them back in your mouth. Once they are out, sure, we can say sorry, we can try to make it right, but it's not easy. Whether you are a past president, or just a normal person, words have a way of standing the test of time.

What are ways that your tongue tends to get you into trouble?

Where do your words help and encourage people?

What people influence the way you speak?

Who is someone you admire for the way he or she speaks to people? Why?

CHAPTER 4: ATTITUDE

Liquid

When I am lost, the search for the street I am looking for can be a stressful time. I tell myself, "It's probably the next road, or the next exit." Oh, I could pull over and ask for help, but that would require actually stopping. There is no time to stop, and after all, I know where I'm going. To stop is a sign of weakness. I'd rather be strong and lost than pull over and admit defeat. Being lost, out of control, or in a hurry doesn't always bring out the best in me. And what I ultimately find out is that it doesn't get me anywhere.

If you are lost while driving, are you a person who stops and asks for directions, or a person who tries to find it on your own?

Play video episode now.

It feels like a bad dream—the kind where you have to ask yourself whether it was a dream or reality. For Natalie, it was real—painfully real. Think about the worst day you have ever had. Everything that is remotely important to you is collapsing all around you. No, not just collapsing, but imploding. You either shut down or lash out—those are pretty much the options. She chose the latter, and it didn't bring out the best in her. Who can blame her? She was living a nightmare.

In what areas of Natalie's life did she need an attitude change?

What things happened to help straighten her out?

[19] My dear brothers and sisters, always be willing to listen and slow to speak. Do not become angry easily, [20] because anger will not help you live the right kind of life God wants. [21] So put out of your life every evil thing and every kind of wrong. Then in gentleness accept God's teaching that is planted in your hearts, which can save you.

[22] Do what God's teaching says; when you only listen and do nothing, you are fooling yourselves. [23] Those who hear God's teaching and do nothing are like people who look at themselves in a mirror. [24] They see their faces and then go away and quickly forget what they looked like. [25] But the truly happy people are those who carefully study God's perfect law that makes people free, and they continue to study it. They do not forget what they heard, but they obey what God's teaching says. Those who do this will be made happy.

[26] People who think they are religious but say things they should not say are just fooling themselves. Their "religion" is worth nothing. [27] Religion that God accepts as pure and without fault is this: caring for orphans or widows who need help, and keeping yourself free from the world's evil influence.

> What does James say about how we should live? What are the results of living/not living this way?

CULTURAL AND HISTORICAL THOUGHTS:

James compares looking into God's Word with looking into a mirror. With God's Word, people either walk away and forget what it says, or they make changes based on what they read. Similarly, people either see imperfections when they look in mirrors but do nothing to fix them, or they use the mirror as a guide to fix the problem. In James' day, mirrors weren't as prolific as they are today. For someone to look in a mirror, he or she had to seek one out. So to go out of one's way to look at oneself, to see imperfections and simply walk away, would be considered ridiculous. It would be the same to look into God's Word for insight, find what you were looking for, and then turn from it without making any adjustments.

We are always on the go. We not only burn the candle at both ends, but we burn it in the middle as well. We are worn-out, burned-out, exhausted. Think about two of the fastest-growing industries in the country: energy drinks and coffee. If we don't have the energy to keep going, we'll find our way through caffeine. I'm as guilty as anyone else. And I write about this passionately because I live it every day. Stop and listen to God? I will tomorrow, when I slow down.

What are some reasons people struggle to stop and listen to God?

What keeps people from listening and acting on what they hear?

It's hard to listen and be slow to speak. I have so much to say! If I listen, how are you going to get to hear what I have to say to you? How are you going to receive all of my incredible wisdom? I have so much to teach, so many points to make. I'm just trying to help. Now that I think about it, why would God want me to stop speaking when I'm doing so much good? This passage in James must be directed to someone else, not me. Or am I not listening again?

What is an area of this passage that God is prompting you to not only listen to, but do something about?

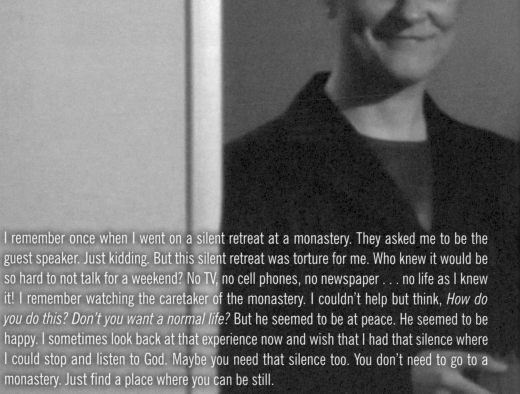

I remember once when I went on a silent retreat at a monastery. They asked me to be the guest speaker. Just kidding. But this silent retreat was torture for me. Who knew it would be so hard to not talk for a weekend? No TV, no cell phones, no newspaper . . . no life as I knew it! I remember watching the caretaker of the monastery. I couldn't help but think, *How do you do this? Don't you want a normal life?* But he seemed to be at peace. He seemed to be happy. I sometimes look back at that experience now and wish that I had that silence where I could stop and listen to God. Maybe you need that silence too. You don't need to go to a monastery. Just find a place where you can be still.

Make a list of how God wants us to live. What are some reasons people struggle to live that way?

What are times when we see people living a godly life?

What keeps us from stopping and listening to God?

What are reasons people don't do what they hear God telling them to do?

When was a time you really felt as if you listened to God and acted upon it? Why did you make the choice to follow God's coaxing? Are you in a place in your life where you would make the same decision now?

CHAPTER 5: FAITH AND WORKS

I'm thinking about some of the great duos of all time: Bogart and Bacall, Montana and Rice, Lennon and McCartney. Or what about some of the great food combinations: chocolate and peanut butter, macaroni and cheese, ice cream and sprinkles? And then there are the foods that go with our favorite activities: movies and popcorn, baseball and hot dogs, girl's night out and chocolate. All of these are dynamic duos. One without the other would be good, but not the same.

What is your favorite duo of all time?

Play video episode now.

We all have dreams, things we want to accomplish, but often we don't go for them. We don't even try to pull them off. Maybe we're too scared, or we can't afford it, or maybe there's just not enough time. People will say it's good enough to dream, or think about doing it. Not for me. If I have a dream, I want to go for it. Now sometimes we do the opposite—we go too far. We want to accomplish something so badly that we cross the line. Like Natalie. She wanted to make a splash, right a wrong, get to the next step in life. But "hijacking" the airwaves may have been a little much. We need to do "works," but maybe it's better to say "good works."

How did Natalie go about things the right way?

The wrong way?

14 My brothers and sisters, if people say they have faith, but do nothing, their faith is worth nothing. Can faith like that save them? 15 A brother or sister in Christ might need clothes or food. 16 If you say to that person, "God be with you! I hope you stay warm and get plenty to eat," but you do not give what that person needs, your words are worth nothing. 17 In the same way, faith that is alone—that does nothing—is dead.

18 Someone might say, "You have faith, but I have deeds." Show me your faith without doing anything, and I will show you my faith by what I do. 19 You believe there is one God. Good! But the demons believe that, too, and they tremble with fear.

20 You foolish person! Must you be shown that faith that does nothing is worth nothing? 21 Abraham, our ancestor, was made right with God by what he did when he offered his son Isaac on the altar. 22 So you see that Abraham's faith and the things he did worked together. His faith was made perfect by what he did. 23 This shows the full meaning of the Scripture that says: "Abraham believed God, and God accepted Abraham's faith, and that faith made him right with God." And Abraham was called God's friend. 24 So you see that people are made right with God by what they do, not by faith only.

What do you learn from this passage about faith and actions (good works)?

CULTURAL AND HISTORICAL THOUGHTS:

James wrote to Christians from a Jewish background. Jews believed that works, rituals, sacrifices, and keeping the law were the way to get to heaven. These new Christians had just discovered the glory of salvation by faith. They knew the exhilaration of receiving righteousness without works, but they then went to the other extreme of thinking that works didn't matter at all. James tried to help Christians strike a balance between the two.

James used examples from the Old Testament that his audience would be familiar with in order to illustrate the concept of faith and actions working together to produce true faith. James brought up the story of Abraham, who was asked to sacrifice his son. Despite Abraham's fear and doubts, he laid Isaac on the altar, demonstrating both faith—believing that God would save him—and action—producing his son for sacrifice.

It's hard to watch the news. It seems that all the stories are about tragedy and heartbreak. But that's not how life is, because in life there is good news and there is bad news. It's the same thing with the Christian life—I have some good news and I have some bad news. The good news is that faith matters. Trusting, leaning, and believing in God are the most important things. The bad news is that there is more to the equation. Though you do not have to work for your salvation, you must work for the kingdom.

When have you seen a situation that displayed faith without actions?

What about actions without faith?

This week was my twelve-year wedding anniversary. I asked my wife what she wanted, and she said, "Nothing." I'm not that dumb, because if I've learned something in twelve years, it's that "nothing" means "something." So I got her a gift and a dozen red roses. I could have gone home and just told her I loved her, but it wouldn't have been enough. I needed to do something to show her. Unless, of course, I wanted to sleep on the couch.

As you look at your life, what do you think you need more of—faith or action?

What would that look like for you?

God says, "You might love me and believe in me, but will you show me that you love me and live for me?" Think of Abraham—he didn't just tell God he trusted him; he was willing to actually show it. Noah built a boat; Moses led the people. All are examples of faith lived out. Have you ever tried to go for one without the other? It doesn't work. We have all probably tried at one time or another, but it just seems as though there's a missing ingredient.

If people were to look at your life, would they say you are a person of incredible faith, or a person of action?

Where do the actions in your life not correspond to your faith?

Do you feel that one (faith or works) is easier than the other? Why?

Do you feel as though the world seems to put more weight in one (faith or works) over the other? Why?

How can we strike a balance between faith and action?

When have you seen actions as a result of faith taken too far?

LEADER'S GUIDE

▬ NOTE TO LEADERS

As leaders, we have tried to make this experience as easy for you as possible. Don't try to do too much during your time together as a group—just ask and listen, and direct when necessary.

The questions have a flow, a progression, and are designed to get people talking. If you help the group start talking early on, they will continue to talk. You will notice that the questions start out easy and casual, creating a theme. The theme continues throughout the session, flowing through casual topics, then into world affairs, and then they begin getting personal.

When the questions ask about the Bible, spend time there. Dig in and scour the passage. Keep looking. You and your group will discover that looking into the Bible can be fun and interesting. Maybe you already know that, but there will be people in your group who don't—people who are afraid of their Bibles, or who don't think they can really study them.

Remember, we are seeking life change. This will happen by taking God's Word and applying it to your life, and to the lives of the people you are with. That's the goal for each person in the group. Fight for it.

■ TIPS

So, are you a little nervous? Guess what—I get scared too. I always have a little apprehension when it comes to leading a group. It's what keeps me on my toes! Here are some things to keep in mind as you're preparing.

Think about your group. How does this week's topic relate to your group? Is this going to be an easy session? Is this going to be a challenge? The more at ease you are with the topic, the better the experience will be for your group.

Go over the leader's material early, and try to get to know the questions. Sometimes there are multiple questions provided at the end of the chapters. These are extra questions that can be used as supplemental questions at any point throughout the discussion. Look over these extra questions and see if any of them jump out at you. Don't feel that you have to address each question, but they are there if you need them. My worst nightmare is to be leading a group and, with thirty minutes still left on the clock, we run out of questions and there's nothing left to talk about . . . so we sit there and stare at one another in painful silence.

Just remember to keep moving through all the questions. The most important goal of this study is to get personal and see how to apply biblical truths to your own life. When you're talking about how a passage plays out in the world today, a common mistake is to not take it deep enough . . . not to push the envelope and move it from what "they" should do to what "I" should do. As a leader, you will struggle with how much to push, how deep to dig. Sometimes it will be just right; sometimes you will push too hard, or sometimes not hard enough. Though it can be nerve-racking, it's the essence of being a leader.

Here are a few more tips:

- Get them talking, laughing, and having fun.
- Don't squelch emotion. Though it may tend to make you uncomfortable, to the point where you'll want to step in and rescue the moment, remember that leaders shouldn't always interfere.
- Jump in when needed. If the question is tough, make sure to model the answer. Try to be open about your own life. Often, the group will only go as deep as you are willing to go.
- When you look in the Bible for answers, don't quit too soon. Let people really search.
- Don't be afraid of quiet.
- Lead the group—don't dominate it.

These are just a few things to think about before you begin.

CHAPTER 1: BAD DAY

> When was a time recently that you had to show restraint or patience with someone?

This should be a fun and easy question for your group to answer. They should have many instances this week where they wanted to explode or yell at someone, but instead managed to respond with patience and restraint. Maybe someone in your group faced a huge challenge at work with a coworker or at school with a classmate, and he or she wanted to rage about it but refrained from responding at all. It will be interesting to hear how your group felt about their responses and if they learned anything from their situations. Question whether they considered their restrained response to be better than if they had yelled or raged at the persons involved.

What does the passage say about troubles and how to respond to them?

A good way to ask this question is to ask it in two parts. First ask, "What does the passage say about troubles in our lives?" James starts by saying that troubles are to be expected (notice it says "when" and not "if") and that these troubles are opportunities for great joy. James also says that when we face troubles, our faith is tested. Give your group a minute or two to consider these facts about troubles or struggles in life.

Tip: If you have people with different Bible translations, read verses 2 and 3 in each translation aloud. Emphasize the different terms used for troubles, such as "trials," "adversities," "struggles," etc.

The passage goes on to say that troubles in our lives present opportunities to develop our endurance to the point of being perfect and complete, needing nothing. God wants us to look at our troubles as a chance to mature and grow in our faith.

Second, ask, "What does the passage say about responding to troubles?" The passage says that we are to ask God for wisdom during these troubles. He won't punish you for asking. He does require that when we ask for wisdom, that our faith be in him alone and that we ask him with the belief that he will answer our requests. We are not to have divided loyalty. We should be unwavering and undivided in our loyalty to him.

How do you see most people viewing their troubles or struggles? How do they respond?

When you look around at people in your office, your school, or even your family and friends, you will see that they tend to view troubles mostly as obstacles, annoyances, or worse—stumbling blocks to faith. They may say, "How can a loving God allow this?" or "If there is a God, why won't he fix this?" We tend to view our troubles as punishments or undeserved penalties. We use struggles in our lives as reasons to quit, excuses for abandoning goals, and a basis for deserting our faith.

Tip: This question may be easier to answer if you think of a particular person in your life who is facing a major struggle. Describe how that person views his or her troubles.

You may want to look at the "both/and" of this question. Think of someone who is facing a struggle and sees it as an obstacle, and then think of someone else who is facing something similar and sees it as an opportunity to watch God work in his or her life.

What troubles are you facing in your life right now, and how will you respond?

Some of your group members may be facing sickness, financial problems, or a struggle with raising a troubled child. It is amazing to think that we are supposed to look at troubles, trials, and struggles with a heart of expectant joy. None of those instances seem like a reason to be joyful, but that's what James says—consider it an opportunity for great joy. Maybe you have a group member who is dealing with a troubled teenager. How would his or her life be different if he or she considered this as an opportunity to grow closer to God by depending on him for wisdom to make brave and righteous choices?

Oftentimes, people pray to God to fix something for them, but they don't think beyond that. It makes such a big difference to believe that God cares, that he is walking through the problem with you, and that he will consistently give you wisdom to face the problem.

Tip: Group members will probably want to spend a lot of time talking about this struggle. Make sure to urge them to respond appropriately. Discuss first how we want to respond, and then look at how God wants us to respond.

As you look back at the struggles in your life, how did you handle them? How did you handle something badly? How did you handle something well? How did it make you stronger?

Who is someone that you admire for how he or she has handled adversity? What made you admire him or her?

How have the struggles in your past influenced and changed you? For the worse? For the better?

How do struggles influence your relationship with God?

Remember, these are optional questions. Use these as you see fit with the group. Using more questions isn't always the answer—sometimes you should just go deeper into those questions that really hit home. But there are times when you need to reach for a few more topics and examine things from a different angle. That's when you can turn to these questions.

CHAPTER 2: TEMPTATIONS

What food is your biggest weakness?

Remember to limit your time on this question so that you'll have time for more important questions. As always, this question is designed to get people talking and to point them to the point of the passage, which is temptation. As you watch this week's episode, have your group watch it through the eyes of "What is tempting for me?"

In the film, what temptation is Natalie facing? What will happen if she gives in? What will happen if she stays strong?

Natalie is faced with the temptation of "fudging" the integrity of the story in order to gain national recognition. By making the doctor look guilty, Natalie gets a more exciting story that will be picked up by networks. It's her chance to really launch her career. It's what every newscaster would want . . . right?

What do you learn about temptation from this passage?

Tip: For purposes of clarity, the definition of temptation is "enticement to evil."

With that in mind, here is what James says about temptation. He says that God blesses people who endure temptation by giving them the crown of life, which is victory over sin, as opposed to people who give in to temptation, which leads to sin or death. Temptation comes from our own desires, not from God. If you succumb, temptation leads to sin. Temptation is not good or perfect, so it can't come from God.

Have your group consider the truths that James tells us to remember: God is good all the time. God gives good gifts. God never changes. God never entices anyone to evil. God gives us desires, but not temptations. God gave us his true Word—Jesus. We are God's prized possession.

What is the process of desire, temptation, defeat, and victory?

Pick different struggles that people might deal with, and break down what this process would look like for each struggle:

At what point is a line crossed? What would happen if people gave in to those temptations? What would happen if people trusted God?

Tip: It's possible you will spend the majority of the time with your group on these questions above. Take 35–40 minutes to answer this particular question. It's a great exercise to understand the process of temptation—analyzing how a harmless desire can turn into something so deceitful.

It is important that your group understands that there is a clear process that leads from desires (not bad) to temptation (can be bad) to sin (bad). Use the following equation with your group to help understand the process.

Desire leads to **temptation** (enticement to evil). This leads us to make a **decision** to either **act on the sin**, which leads to **death**, or **act on endurance and trust**, which leads to **life**.

Remember, the line at times can be gray; the line can be different for different people. This is not the time to get bogged down on where the line might be. The question is designed to look at the world, and to talk about the temptations we are faced with. It is important to point out that there is a difference between being tempted and crossing the line.

The final part of the question asks you to compare and contrast giving in to temptation and trusting in God.

What is an area in your life in which you feel tempted but don't cross the line? What is an area in which temptation is leading you over the line? Why do you think you experience strength in one area and not the other?

What are truths from the passage that can help you deal with not giving in to temptation?

These are the kind of questions in which you need to really know your group in order to have a successful discussion. These are tough questions. If you are in a same-sex group, it may be easier for people to answer. If you don't feel your group is ready to be asked these questions, pick some of the optional questions to use during this time. Perhaps you could end the group with these questions, but do it in a way where they take it to God in prayer, rather than share with the group. Err on the side of caution.

What do you think makes certain things in life more tempting than others?

How does the world work hard at trying to tempt us?

What is an area of temptation that you have overcome? What helped you to overcome it?

When do you feel most tempted in life?

What are things you do to help deal with temptation?

Tip: Remember, these are extra questions for you to use as you see fit. Get to know the questions, and place them in the study where you feel they may be appropriate. Try to use them in a casual way. Also, remember that asking more questions isn't always better. Try to dig deeper and spend more time on the questions you ask. That helps people really share what is on their hearts.

CHAPTER 3: WORDS

> **Describe an affirmation or great compliment you've received.**

This should be a fun question to answer with your group. People receive compliments for all different aspects of their lives, such as in their appearance, performance, athleticism, intelligence, acts of kindness, talents. Let people boast a little bit as they share compliments they've received.

Tip: Because we are focusing on the power of the spoken word, it is important for your group to think about how they felt after they received the affirmation or compliment, so you may have to follow up their answers with a second question. A good way to do this would be to say, "That's an amazing compliment. How did you feel when they said that?"

What do you learn about the tongue and its effects from this passage?

In the first couple of verses, James tells us that if we become teachers of the Bible, we will be judged more strictly. The words of a Bible teacher are important because they influence others in their faith. The words these teachers choose must not only meet speech standards, but standards of truth and consistency with God's Word.

In this passage James uses a lot of comparative descriptions, therefore, it is a good idea to not just read the words, but to briefly discuss their meaning. For instance, James compares the tongue to controlling a large horse with a small bit, or a huge ship with a small rudder. He says that the tongue is a small thing that we use to make grand speeches. James is saying there is a lot of power behind that small thing.

James continues in verses 5 and 6 and compares the tongue to a spark, flame, and forest fire. The tongue can corrupt your entire body, and it can set your whole life on fire. He says our tongues are set on fire "by hell itself." Satan uses our tongues for his purposes—damage, division, destruction. Consider a forest fire: how quickly it moves, the destruction it causes, the years it takes to regenerate life in its aftermath.

In verses 7 and 8 James compares controlling what we say to taming all kinds of animals, birds, reptiles, and fish. When you consider the incredible task of taming animals—for example, a killer whale named Shamu—and the concentrated effort and daily discipline that takes, James is saying that we can't accomplish that with our own tongues. He says our tongue is restless and evil, full of deadly poison.

In the final verses James talks about contradictory speech. He says the same mouth that praises God, curses those made in his image. But blessings and cursing cannot come from the same tongue. He compares this absurdity to a spring of water producing both fresh and bitter water, and a fig tree producing olives, and a grapevine producing figs.

What situations or places tend to bring out the worst or best in people's tongues?

Some situations or places that bring out the worst in people's language could be sports competitions, nightclubs, college fraternity parties, high-pressure offices. Consider also mentioning lying, slandering, and gossiping, as those are ways people use and abuse their tongues.

Some examples of places that bring out the best in people's language could be church, family gatherings, or other places where children are present.

Tip: The tendency here may be to immediately talk only about either the worst or best. Make sure your group considers both sides of this question.

Where have you seen the effects of someone's words? What is a positive example? What about a negative example?

First, refer briefly to the passage where James says that the tongue is like a forest fire. Reemphasize the damage it can do. Lead your group to talk about the damage they've seen produced by someone's word choice. Maybe they have witnessed criticism at work and how it damaged the employee's self-confidence. Perhaps they have witnessed, or even personally experienced, verbal abuse by a parent and its destructive results.

Next, remind your group that James says that blessings also pour from our mouths. Ask them what effects they've seen from people choosing encouraging, positive, and supportive words. One example would be encouraging a child in a sport, which resulted in the child persevering and become really good at the sport. It could also be the exemplary work turned in by an employee who has been praised for effort and performance.

What situations or places in your life seem to bring out the worst in your tongue?

Tip: Allow enough time for each member of your group to be able to answer this question. As the leader, you may want to share first.

Group members should be able to think of areas where they have problems controlling their tongue—such as using harsh words when they become angry at their children, criticizing a co-worker who has messed up, cursing in a competitive game of basketball or other sport, or gossiping with friends.

This may be very convicting for some of your group members, and they may get emotional while they answer. Continue to encourage them as they share. You may want to say, "I know this is hard. We all struggle with our words and the damage they can do. Thank you for being so honest with all of us."

Where in your life can you use your words in a positive way? What effect would this have on your life and on those around you?

Tip: You may want to ask the above questions together. As someone shares a situation where he or she has trouble controlling the tongue, you could ask, "What would change if you didn't respond with anger or hurtful words to your child, but instead used your words in a positive way?" or, "What would change if you didn't join in the gossip with your friends, but instead changed the subject altogether?" Let your group spend a minute discussing the effects of positive words that encourage, praise, and show love.

What are some ways that your tongue tends to get you into trouble?

When do your words help and encourage people?

Which people influence the way you speak?

Who is someone you admire for the way he or she speaks to people? Why?

Tip: These may be just slight variations to prior questions. Keep these in your "back pocket," and use when appropriate. As you get to know your group better and better, always look over the questions first and see which ones work best for them. Use these questions if you feel your group needs further prodding, or if conversation stalls.

CHAPTER 4: ATTITUDE

> If you are lost while driving, are you a person who stops and asks for directions, or a person who tries to find it on your own?

Only spend a couple of minutes on this question, as you will be spending a large amount of time on question 3. Let people tell some stories about when they were lost and wouldn't stop to ask directions.

In what areas of Natalie's life did she need an attitude change? What things happened to help straighten her out?

Natalie is having her world collapse around her. She is feeling overwhelmed and a bit out of control. It takes her stopping and getting guidance from an unlikely source, Chip, to get some perspective. She realized he was right when he told her to "quit being so angry." Now, she not only has to listen to him, but to do something about what he said.

What does James say about how we should live? What are the results from living/not living this way?

It may be best to make a list of the "how we should live" areas first, then write next to them the results from living or not living this way.

How to live: listen to God; hear and do what he says; be calm and patient; control your anger; think before speaking; get rid of filth; be humble; accept God's Word; control pride and arrogance

Results: a righteous life that God desires; being saved by God; freedom; blessings; a right perspective on life (taking care of orphans and widows)

What are some reasons people struggle to stop and listen to God?

What keeps people from listening and acting on what they hear?

James gives us quite a list of how God wants us to live. Ask people to share some of the difficulties involved in living this way. For example, some people have trouble stopping and listening. Ask the group why they think this is. Remember not to make this about the individuals in the group yet. Save the more personal direction for the next question. Remember that whenever we look at how people live, it is always important to not be critical. Keep the discussion as general as possible.

What is an area of the passage that God is prompting you to not only listen to, but to do something about?

Refer back to your list on "How to live."

Tip: This is a good question for you, as the leader, to answer first. Here's an example of how you could model answering the question: "Wow, after looking at this list, I feel so convicted about watching my tongue. I have such a tendency to fly off the handle when dealing with people. I say things I regret, even though I know I can control it, because there are times I do. God is really prompting me as I read this passage to make big changes in that area of my life. What about you? Was there something we talked about tonight where God was prompting you? Was there something that resonated with you, where you would really like to make some changes in your actions?"

This may seem overwhelming to your group, because people could be struggling in several different areas. Help your group realize that God doesn't expect them to change everything all at once. God only wants you to take on as much as you can handle, one area at a time.

The main goal of this exercise is to recognize God's prompting in our lives. Hold up the mirror to the group and help group members acknowledge their imperfections. Don't let them deny they exist.

CHAPTER 5: FAITH AND WORKS

What is your favorite duo of all time?

Encourage your group to think of great pairings of people and things, such as great acting duos that seemed better together than when separate, such as Lewis and Martin, or musical duos, such as Sonny and Cher. Or you could go another direction and think about food or activity duos. Have them defend why any of these people or things are better together than alone.

How did Natalie go about things the right way? The wrong way?

Natalie had a passion: she wanted to make a difference, to make a big splash. But she didn't just keep that passion hidden inside—she lived it out. The problem is, Natalie may have gone a little too far. This could be a time to talk about having the right heart, but going about things the wrong way.

What do you learn from this passage about faith and actions (good works)?

Dig for several observations from this passage. Not only will you see clear definitions, but you will also see some great illustrations. You have Abraham and Rahab, great stories of faith and works lived out. Specifically talk about those two people to illustrate your point of faith and works. Concentrate on the fact that both faith and works are essential to the Christian life.

When have you seen a situation that displayed faith without actions? What about actions without faith?

It is easy to look around and see people who promote a lot of good deeds—feeding the poor, giving money to fund AIDS research, or standing up for the marginalized, but their foundation is not their faith in Christ. On the other hand, it is easy to think of examples of people we know who attend church and seem to be faithful, but they somehow hear the plea to help those in need and walk away without a second glance. They don't seem to demonstrate their faith other than by talking about it. On a more positive note, there are those who do both. Think of some examples of people who demonstrate both faith and action.

Tip: Steer your group away from using names of people in their answers. They can refer to family members, friends, etc, but in a generic sort of way. That way you will prevent gossip and promote learning.

As you look at your life, what do you need more of—faith or action? What would that look like for you?

With this question, you are encouraging members to assess their lives, to stop and think, *How do I really live this out?* We all tend to steer one direction more than another. At the same time, this is also a great time to affirm the areas in your lives, or in others' lives, where you see great faith and great works, or best of all, both faith and works lived out. We often tend to look at just the negative, so make sure you do not beat yourself up, but look for the positive, too.

If people were to look at your life, would they say you are a person of faith, or a person of action?

In what areas of your life do your actions not correspond to your faith?

Do you feel as though one (faith or works) is easier than the other? Why?

Do you feel as if the world seems to put more weight on one (faith or works) over the other? Why?

How can we strike a balance between faith and action?

When have you seen actions as a result of faith taken too far?

Tip: Use these questions where you feel appropriate. Use them to supplement other questions that you use throughout the study. Remember, the world may put more weight on one over the other, but God says that both faith and works are essential.

LIQUID would love to thank:

Chris Marcus, for being a producer, designer, editor, and director of photography on the project. You did it all, and we could not have done it without you.

Mariners Church: To the staff and small group department for all of their help and insight into this entire project. And to the congregation and elder board for their prayers and support.

Kenton Beshore, for the beauty of flow questions.

All of the incredible people in North Carolina, who got this whole thing started.

The cast and crew, for the endless hours of hard work and incredible performances.

Aaron and Mark of Tank Creative, for making us sound good.

Cindy Western, for her help in crafting great questions.

Our incredible editor, Kim Hearon, who, to put it simply, had to deal with us. You made it fun.

All the people at Thomas Nelson, for your hard work and expertise.

And we thank God for having his hand on this project and blessing it.